7-FIGURE HEALTHY HABITS

HOW TO CREATE HEALTHY HABITS

FOR SUCCESS

LENAE GOOLSBY, JD & TRIP GOOLSBY, MD

TABLE OF CONTENTS

Introduction

Acknowledgements

INTRODUCTION

It's been said that successful people are just ordinary people with extraordinary habits. This might seem somewhat over-simplified.

Many of us were either taught or through various life experiences, or even from early influencer imprinting, came to believe that success is a rare combination of talents that only a few people are lucky enough to be born with. We all know someone we perceive as "successful," but perhaps we just can't quite put our finger on why they are as successful as they are.

Could it just be the right habits?

Possibly, but it is not just having the "right" or positive habits. It is also about mindfully shifting away from, or not actively choosing the "bad" or negative habits, too.

"Unsuccessful" people are just as skilled, but they are also skilled at missing opportunities for success by engaging in habits that simply do not serve them.

It is our habits that ultimately determine our success.

The good news is that habits are learned behaviors.
Just as you learned to brush your teeth or get out of bed each morning, you can learn 7-Figure Healthy Habits to create your own success.

Look, it took a while to create the habits that you have, so be patient with yourself as you begin to choose to release those habits which no longer serve you and embrace new habits that do.

Before we get started, let's consider what a habit actually is.

The dictionary defines a "Habit" as "A settled or regular tendency or practice, especially one that is hard to give up." So, a habit is just something that you do regularly. You do it with little mental effort, like brushing your teeth.

Making 100 cold calls each day can be a habit. But being miserable throughout the process suggests that it's not a true habit, since it would be easy to give up.

So, we are not just talking about doing something useful on a regular basis, we are talking about making it a comfortable part of your routine.

ACKNOWLEDGMENTS

Thank you to the patient-partners of Infinite Health Integrative Medicine Center. Your willingness to step up, show-up and do what it takes to take your health power back to be successful, not just in your health goals, but also, by natural extension, you career, relationship, and spiritual growth goals, as well, is what encourages us to keep serving our communities.

Thank you to the team of Infinite Health, as well. We could not be of service in the way that we are without your dedication, not just to the patient-partners and the mission and vision of the organization, but also towards yourself.

Thank you to the readers of this and other publications of ours. May you be blessed with the success in your life that you desire and that is your birth-right.

1.

THE 7-FIGURE HEALTHY HABITS

"We can use decision-making to choose the habits we want to form, use willpower to get the habit started, then - and this is the best part – we can allow the extraordinary power of habit to take over. At that point, we're free from the need to decide and the need to use willpower." - Gretchen Rubin

Each successful person has a unique set of habits, habits that are healthy because they serve the goals and the agendas of the 7-Figure earners. While some healthy habits are individual to the pursuit of the 7-Figure earner, other healthy habits are general, or most common to those who may be considered "successful."

If one of your goals is to create healthy habits that actually serve and honor you so that you can step in to a "successful" life, whether that looks like a 7-Figure income, or a healthier, fitter body, or perhaps more loving relationships, these habits are a great starting point for creating real change in your life.

Create a core list of 7-Figure Healthy Habits and then add the necessary habits that fit your needs. By adopting these habits, you will find yourself becoming more successful, too.

Consider these habits, but avoid viewing this list as exhaustive. Feel free to add to it as you see fit.

Have a target. You would not leave your home without a destination in mind. You would never arrive if you did not know where you were going to start with.

Setting goals is a huge part of success. It would be challenging to find a highly successful person that couldn't recite their goals to you on command.

DO YOU HAVE GOALS? IF NOT, WHY NOT?

SUCCESSFUL PEOPLE ARE PROACTIVE

Those who are successful CHOOSE what they want to happen rather than merely take whatever comes their way. When they see that something needs to be done, they do it.

Unsuccessful people are reactive. They react to whatever life throws their way. They do not do things that need to be done until forced by a dwindling timeline. Rather, they just hope for the best.

EXERCISE

There are many out of shape successful people, but interestingly, the vast majority of them do engage in regular exercise. Many of them choose to perform their exercise in the morning while others are still asleep.

This is an example of doing what needs to be done, and doing it consistently.

THOSE THAT ARE SUCCESSFUL TAKE PERSONAL RESPONSIBILITY FOR THEIR LIVES.

They also take responsibility for a lot of other things, too.

The average person would rather find excuses and push responsibilities onto others.

When you are responsible, you can change anything in your life. You do not have to wait for luck, or for someone else to do it for you.

A PREMIUM IS PLACED ON TIME

7-Figure people appreciate the value of their energy and accordingly of the value of their time. They are constantly trying to find ways to leverage their time.

Try getting someone ultra-successful to give you 10 minutes of their time - it better be worth it.

The average person views their time as worth a certain amount of money per hour, whereas a 7-Figure person is always trying to increase the value of their time.

THE ABILITY TO MANAGE EMOTIONAL STATES IS PARAMOUNT

7-Figure people excel at managing their emotional states on a consistent basis. They make level-headedness a habit. They make decisions with their brains, not their emotions.

The average person has the habit of being controlled by his emotional state, and reacting from whatever emotional state is present moment to moment.

USE FAILURE WISELY

7 Figure people use failure as a learning tool and as motivation. They have a habit for dealing with failure in a certain way. This "dealing-with-failure habit" doesn't include quitting or feeling dejected.

A person of average success uses failure as an excuse to give up.

PRIORITIZATION

Those that accomplish a lot have a habit of focusing on the most important things. It doesn't matter if they feel like doing it. They just do it because it's the logical thing to do.

What does the average person do? They have a habit of doing the tasks in order from most enjoyable to least. They'll put off the least enjoyable tasks until the last possible moment.

FOCUS ON IMPROVEMENT

7-Figure people are concerned with improvement. They know that a little improvement adds up to a lot over time.

Perfection is the enemy of progress.

The average person wants to do it perfectly. They also lack the patience to accumulate small improvements. They want instant gratification.

These are general habits shared by most 7 Figure people. Habits can be much more specific. For example, a successful real estate agent would have a different set of habits than a professional athlete.

There are many habits that can make you more successful. Consider the habits that would be most useful to your goals and your general life. You might come up with a few

better options for yourself. Take a few
minutes to compile a list of habits that
would be most useful for you.

2.

HOW TO CREATE A NEW 7-FIGURE HEALTY HABIT

"Make no mistake about it. Bad habits are called 'bad' for a reason. They kill our productivity and creativity. They slow us down. They hold us back from achieving our goals. And they're detrimental to our health." - John Rampton

You already know that new habits may not necessarily be particularly easy to instill, after all you may have to "re-write" decades of old habits that no longer serve.

However, with an effective process, you can accomplish nearly anything. Instead of attempting to force yourself to create new behaviors in your life, you may choose to utilize a more methodical approach. By becoming an adept and creating new habits that actually serve, you become empowered.

TRY THESE PROCESSES TO HELP YOU DEVELOP AN EFFECTIVE COMBINATION OF HABITS TO SUCCEED:

WHAT DO YOU WANT? Identify the habit you want to create. (Let's use exercising daily at the gym for 40 minutes, as an example.

WHY DO YOU WANT IT? Know WHY you want to create this habit. What will you gain? What are the advantages. Think long and short-term. Give your brain a good reason to want to go to the gym.

WHAT ARE YOU WILLING TO GIVE (OR GIVE UP) TO RECEIVE IT?

Identify the cost of not creating this habit. What pain will you endure if you don't exercise regularly? An unattractive figure? Low self-esteem? Poor health? An early death?

DETERMINE THE LOWEST LEVEL OF THE HABIT

Let's use exercising daily at the gym as an example. You want to make the habit easy to accomplish. The hardest part of working out at the gym is just getting there. So, the lowest level of this habit might be to get to the gym and exercise for one minute. That's it.

If that proves to be too challenging, make it even easier. You just have to set foot inside the gym.

SET YOURSELF UP FOR SUCCESS

There are things you can do to make it easier to go to the gym. A few ideas include:

- ✓ Choosing a gym that is close to your home or work.
- ✓ Packing your gym bag the night before.
- ✓ Choosing a form of exercise that you like.
- ✓ Finding a workout partner.
- ✓ Choosing a convenient time of day.
- ✓ Renting a locker at the gym to keep some things there readily available.

CHOOSE A TRIGGER

A trigger is something that you do right before you perform the habit. It might be walking out to your car in the morning or after work. It might be saying goodbye to the receptionist at work on your way out the door.

Think about when you brush your teeth. You perform that task right after doing something else. It might be turning off the hall light, shaving, or availing yourself of the facilities, but you have a trigger.

DETERMINE A TRIGGER FOR YOUR HABIT

If possible, perform your habit daily. Every-other day habits are more difficult to implement. Weekly habits are even more challenging to implement.

CELEBRATE WHEN YOU ARE SUCCESSFUL

Remember, for this example, getting to the gym and exercising for one minute is success. Be excited! Jump up and down like you just won an Olympic marathon! The key is to make yourself feel good, so you're more likely to go to the gym again.

BE PATIENT

The largest study done on habit formation found that it took an average of 66 days to create a habit. While that is the average, there are a few people who can create a new habit in less time, while others may take even longer. The key here is to be patient with yourself.

You may have heard that it takes 28 to 30 days to form a new habit, but that's not supported in the scientific literature. Be prepared for your new habit to take a while to sink in.

Remember, the initial focus is on creating the lowest level of the habit. The important thing is making a habit of getting yourself to the gym. The actual exercising will tend to take care of itself.

Positive changes in your life will occur more rapidly if you have supporting habits in place. Rather than being a slave to your habits, develop habits that serve your desires. When the right behaviors become automatic, your success will be automatic, too.

3.

HOW TO RELEASE HABITS THAT NO LONGER SERVE

"Times of transition are strenuous, but I love them. They are an opportunity to purge, rethink priorities, and be intentional about new habits. We can make our new normal any way we want." - Kristin Armstrong

Consciously creating habits that serve you is a valuable skill to have, but the ability to eliminate performing habits that do not serve you is just as important.

Habits that do not serve you, are simply not setting you up for success and can feel like they are actually making your life more difficult than it has should be.

Holding on to habits that do not serve for short-term gains, is actually contrary to success. Maybe you have heard Financial "guru," Dave Ramsey say, *"You have to live like no one else today, so you can live like no one else tomorrow."* This is the discipline of a 7-Figure person.

RELEASE YOUR BAD HABITS AND SET YOURSELF FREE WITH THESE PROCESSES:

Consider your goals and list those habits that are interfering with you reaching your goals. Consider the far-reaching effects of the habits that are not serving you.

For example, overeating can interfere not only with your health and appearance goals, but can also interfere with your ability to play with your children.

You might enlist the help of your partner or close friends. They can probably offer some interesting and beneficial insights.

PICK A JUST ONE OR TWO HABITS
TO ADDRESS.

Either choose to release the habit that is having the greatest negative impact on your life, or choose a habit that will be easy to break. Either make a significant change or allow yourself to gain momentum.

Determine the benefit you're gaining from that habit. Keep in mind that your negative habits are providing you with some type of reward, otherwise you wouldn't be doing them.

Think about how you feel before performing the habit and how you feel afterwards. What do you get from taking this action that you know isn't in your best interest?

FIND ANOTHER WAY TO GET THE SAME BENEFIT

How can you get the same benefit without harming yourself or your life? List a few alternative behaviors that you believe would be effective substitutes and begin making a positive habit out of the best option.

What happens right before you perform the habit? What are the circumstances that trigger your habit?

- ✓ Is it a certain time of day?
- ✓ A stressful interaction at work?
- ✓ Stress in general?
- ✓ Spending time with a certain friend?
- ✓ Loneliness?
- ✓ Fatigue?

When possible, avoid the triggers that are most likely to initiate your non-serving habit. Maybe watching TV late at night leads to overeating. It would make sense to find another activity to keep occupied at night. Do your best to find a way around your triggers and your habit will be easier to overcome.

INSTALL A BETTER HABIT

This is critical to your success. Create a new habit to replace the habit that is not serving you. It is not enough to tell yourself that you'll meditate instead of smoking. It is necessary to make a habit of meditating regularly.

It is not enough to think your way past a habit you know you want to release. It is necessary to train yourself to shift or pivot away from it and towards a new more self-honoring behavior.

Once again, be patient with yourself. Remember that changing your behavior is an undertaking, it may be a bit challenging. Allow for missteps and forgive yourself if you "backslide." Simply observe it, without judgment, and redirect your focus back to your new choice. If you have to do this over and over and over again, it is OKAY.

Our lives are largely determined by the number and magnitude of our non-serving habits. Eliminating these self-imposed anchors is an important skill to develop. Perhaps in the past these habits provided temporary comfort, and they may be somewhat difficult to eliminate. If needed, briefly remind yourself of the damage being caused by these habits, imagine your life with your new, more honoring habits and keep moving forward.

Another important skill to develop is the ability to deal with discomfort. Your ability to handle stress and other emotional discomfort is closely matched to your ability to drop your bad habits. How do you handle stress? How can you better handle stress?

CONCLUSION

"It seems, in fact, as though the second half of a man's life is made up of nothing, but the habits he has accumulated during the first half." - Fyodor Dostoevsky

The world's most impressive people gained that distinction through their habits. Whether you want to be wealthy, healthy, wise, or all three, you can use a role model and adopt their habits. Take advantage of modeling after someone else's success – there is no need to reinvent the wheel.

Take a look at your goals and the type of person you want to become. Who has accomplished those things? It might be someone from history or your next-door neighbor. Ask them, if possible, what positive habits they consistently perform. How do they spend their day? What do they eat? How much do they sleep? What are their investing, spending, saving habits? Ask powerful questions, then create a list of the habits you want to incorporate into your life and then get started… today… right now… there is zero need to wait.

It may feel like "old habits die hard," but they can be overcome. New, self-serving and honoring habits may take a bit to implement develop, but you can and if you so choose, you will.

ABOUT THE AUTHORS

 **Trip Goolsby, MD**, a New Thought Leader in Integrative Medicine, is the CEO/Cofounder of Infinite Health Integrative Medicine Center, an elite precision medicine practice with a niche focus on health optimization, longevity and regenerative medicines. He is a bestselling author, having coauthored "Success in the New Economy" with Bryan Tracy and other industry experts. He and his wife, LeNae Goolsby, JD wrote "Empowered Medicine: Harnessing the laws of the universe for optimized health," which is the Bible of Infinite Health, and one of the five pillars of their approach to health optimization. For over 30 years Dr. Goolsby has helped thousands of patients, across the globe, live longer, healthier, happier lives.

 **LeNae Goolsby, JD** is the cofounder of Infinite Health, as well as an empowerment-centric bestselling author, speaker and consultant. In addition to co-authoring, "Empowered Medicine," LeNae is the author of "Seven Sundays to Sweet Inner Serenity: How to cultivate the calm even in the midst of the crazy chaos," and co-author of "Empowered Living." She, along with her husband, Trip Goolsby, MD reside in New Orleans, Louisiana, with their two sons, and 2.5 dogs.

For more information about LeNae Goolsby, JD & Trip Goolsby, MD and Infinite Health Integrative Medicine Center visit www.YourInfiniteHealth.com

WOULD YOU LIKE TO GET COACHED PERSONALLY BY LENAE GOOLSBY, JD & TRIP GOOLSBY, MD?

An integral pillar of Infinite Health Integrative Medicine, Dr. Goolsby's elite precision medicine integrative practice is "Motivational Medicine." Here is where true transformation is made.

Because of the success of this pillar, Dr. Goolsby and LeNae began offering Motivational Medicine to those who are not able to physically participate in Infinite Health's onsite programs, but still desired to enhance their health and success goals with Dr. Goolsby & LeNae's expertise.

Presently, there are two different coaching programs available:

THE 8-WEEK MILLIONAIRE HEALTH METHOD GROUP COACHING PROGRAM

AND

THE 12 MONTH VIP ONE ON ONE PRIVATE COACHING PROGRAM

Both programs are filled to the brim with value and both require an application for acceptance. To request your application, or for more information, send your email to LeNae.Goolsby@gmail.com and include the name of the coaching program you are interested in the subject line of the email.

One Last Thing...

If you enjoyed this book or found it helpful, we would be very grateful if you would post a short review on Amazon. Your support really does make a difference and we read all the reviews personally so that we can get your feedback to improve future offerings.

www.ingramcontent.com/pod-product-compliance
Lightning Source LLC
Chambersburg PA
CBHW031503210526
45463CB00003B/1052